Quilted
Fairie Tales

Linda M. Poole

American Quilter's Society

P. O. Box 3290 • Paducah, KY 42002-3290
FAX 270-898-1173 *www.americanquilter.com*

Love to Quilt...

Located in Paducah, Kentucky, the American Quilter's Society (AQS) is dedicated to promoting the accomplishments of today's quilters. Through its publications and events, AQS strives to honor today's quiltmakers and their work and to inspire future creativity and innovation in quiltmaking.

Editors: Barbara Smith & Linda Baxter Lasco
Copy Editor: Chrystal Abhalter
Graphic Design: Amy Chase
Cover Design: Michael Buckingham
Quilt Photos: Charles R. Lynch

Library of Congress Cataloging-in-Publication Data

Poole, Linda M.
    Quilted fairie tales : love to quilt series / by Linda M. Poole.
        p. cm.
    Includes bibliographical references and index.
    ISBN 1-57432-913-8
    1. Patchwork quilts. 2. Quilting--Patterns. 3. Fairies in art. I. Title.
    TT835.P6428 2006
    746.46'041--dc22

                                    2006019889

Additional copies of this book may be ordered from the American Quilter's Society, PO Box 3290, Paducah, KY 42002-3290, or call 1-800-626-5420 or online at www.AmericanQuilter.com.

Proudly printed and bound in the
United States of America

Dedication

If words could be the warmth of loving hugs, then volumes of printed words would gently envelop two people I love — my parents, Gloria and Gero Grohs. Without their encouragement and guidance, I would not be who I am today.

Acknowledgments

Without my friends
Of new and old
This fairie tale
Might not be told

ever-ending appreciation goes to my mom, Gloria, and dad, Gero, for teaching me all the things necessary to learn, love, and dream during my childhood and adult years. I love you both with all my heart!

I want to thank my winter mom, Helen Umstead, who gives me honest opinions and dreams the dreams with me while creating, traveling, and quilting the hours away.

Endless hugs go to my good friends Alison Rumble and Michael Smith in the United Kingdom, who opened their home to me to write this book. You both are near and dear to my heart. Ali caught the "quilting bug" and appliquéd her first fairie while I was there—an unexpected surprise!

Without my precious Nashville 5 (Deborah Adams, Janice Breyer, Cheryl L. Robinson-Atwood, Virginia St. John, and LuAnne Williams), I would not be writing this book. Thank you for your curiosity, inventiveness, our newly found friendships, and for allowing each of us to dream aloud.

To the gals on the FairieGoddessMothers list on Yahoo®, I have never met a nicer group of ladies, who nurture one another and keep the quilts and stories alive. You have enriched my life tenfold. Thank you!

To my quilt guild, the Milford Valley Quilters Guild in Milford, Pennsylvania, you have always been there for me through thick and thin, and I thank my friends from the beginning and the friends I have just met.

To Judy Irish for always putting my quilts first.

To Barbara Smith, my editor, who has again worked her magic in helping me birth my third book, I never could ask for a more wonderful editor, friend, or birthing coach.

To the Martini Girls, Joan Shay and Marie Seroskie, you always believed in me. Thank you.

To my eclectic, wacky, and whimsical Retreat Girls, you make me laugh, cry, and let me just be me, hugs to each of you in the castle door.

I also want to thank my sister, Billie Jo Poole, for keeping me organized and for being the dearest friend I will always cherish.

And finally, to the incredible staff of the American Quilter's Society (AQS), you have given me more opportunities than I ever imagined. I will be forever grateful to each of you.

Table of Contents

Foreword

Birth of the FairieGoddessMothers

Once upon a time, not so long ago (August 2003, to be exact), in a fabulous palace (the Gaylord Opryland® Resort & Convention Center in Nashville, Tennessee), there arrived from the north a wise and wonderful FairieGoddessMother named Linda M. Poole. Linda had journeyed many miles, seeking to share her love of fairies and appliqué quilts.

Stepping from her magic carpet, she found a roomful of eager pupils awaiting words of advice and wisdom. Realizing that she had encountered a meeting of like minds, Linda proceeded to share with these mortals the precious, treasured secrets of freezer-paper appliqué.

In the twinkling of an eye, the room was filled with flying needles, colorful fabrics, and dangerously sharp scissors. The very air sparkled with conversation and laughter. In no time at all, something magical happened. From mere fabric and imagination, fabulous fairies came to life. As each developed her own personality, the fanciful creatures demanded that their stories be shared amongst their human creators. And so, the humans began weaving wondrous tales to share.

According to the quilters, one lovely fairie was, in fact, a mermaid in search of an ocean-trapped sailor to bestow her love upon and to forever share her watery paradise. Another fairie, adorned in a fancy dancing dress and toting a guitar, roamed Music Row. She was seeking fame, fortune, and a country music recording contract. One singularly shy sprite, fading into the night shadows, was revealed to spin sweet slumber for weary dreamers with the fluff of forgotten wishes. These stories were only the beginning of the many told that day.

While witnessing the miraculous birth of these fey creatures, the mere mortals noticed a strange tingling on their backs, just between their shoulder blades. Industrious souls that they were, they kept their heads diligently bent to task. Only Linda was able to see the lovely wings sprouting from the backs of her new apprentices. The wise wizard kept her counsel, but flying back to Pennsylvania on her magic carpet, she began to conjure a new spell.

Using the magic of the Internet, FairieGoddessMother Linda sent out a summons far and wide, inviting all and sundry to join her in creating a new flitter of fairies, crafted from fabrics, adorned with embellishments, and flaunting fanciful fairie tales. With the wave of a magic "mouse," Wizard Linda and her apprentices, who are now known as the FairieGoddessMothers, initiated into their ranks fairie lovers from throughout the United States and, indeed, all across the world.

Plans were made for their newly created fabric fairies to travel, to be shared with those seeking beauty, fantasy, and entertainment at quilt shows far and wide. And, perhaps most wonderfully of all, sweet friendship sprang up among dozens of former strangers, now united electronically in a web of fantasy, fun, and creative energy.

We, the FairieGoddessMothers, would like to take this opportunity to throw open the portals of our mystical land of fantasy and beauty. And, so, I bestow upon you these magical words: http://groups.yahoo.com/group/fairiegoddessmothers/.

With the simple stroke of your enchanted keyboard, you, too, can join us, and we shall all live happily ever after!

Cheryl Atwood-Robinson
Cloversport, Kentucky

Next to the doorway of my childhood bedroom was a bookshelf filled with encyclopedias, the *Big Book of Fairy Tales*, the dictionary, an atlas, and hard-covered children books. I loved taking books to bed with me and would read until my eyelids were heavy with sleep. As much as I loved to read children's stories, I began to wonder about the tales a little more in depth.

As young as I was, I just could not understand why a big egg would sit on a wall and fall off, or why people would try to put the egg back together again just so he could go back onto the wall and possibly fall once more. I still question why that little boy Jack had to sit in a corner and stick his thumb into a pie. Where was his mother? I know my mom wouldn't let me sit alone with a whole pie, much less stick my fingers into it. And lastly, remember the guy Peter who was the pumpkin eater? Why couldn't he keep his wife? And why did he put her in a pumpkin shell?

And so, the overactive imagination of an inquisitive little girl stayed with me until adulthood and blessedly got me where I am today, writing for you *Quilted Fairie Tales*.

Fairie Dust

I still find wonderment in everything I do and everything I read. Even when traveling, I cannot help being drawn to the tiniest architectural designs and wonder how an artisan of centuries past found the joy in creating his small masterpieces. I can almost be certain that when the masters of great art painted, their inspirations and stories unfolded beneath their paintbrushes.

Perhaps there isn't always an answer, but there are always questions to be asked, mysteries to wonder about, and stories to write.

Inspiration and Imagination

Inspiration is everywhere you go. It really is that simple. Inspiration finds you when you least expect it or when you open your thoughts to receiving it.

Finding and Capturing Ideas

Carry a camera with you when you travel or take walks, jot down ideas in a small notebook, or sketch the things that inspire you.

Write the word "inspiration" on an accordion folder and label the individual pockets inside with words like flowers, skies, colors, nature, etc. When you're leafing through a magazine and find something that catches your eye, carefully rip the page out and put it into the appropriate spot in your folder. When you're in need of some eye candy, just look through your folder.

One of our greatest resources for inspiration is young children. Within a child's mind, the sky can be any color and the ocean can have fish that fly. Just take a peek through some children's books and you will see that their imaginations are limitless.

Ideas can come naturally by smelling new scents or memorable aromas, hearing a familiar sound like birds singing in the morning, or touching something pleasing like smooth river rocks. These can motivate you to create.

Novelty fabrics can bring a whole new dimension to the world of inspiration. So many of my fairie ideas have been thought up by daydreaming over the variety of novelty fabrics—I am sure to find something that corresponds to my ideas.

Fairie Dust

What works for me is asking myself questions and then answering them with the not so obvious answer. Adding fairies into the answer makes for a delightful fairie tale.

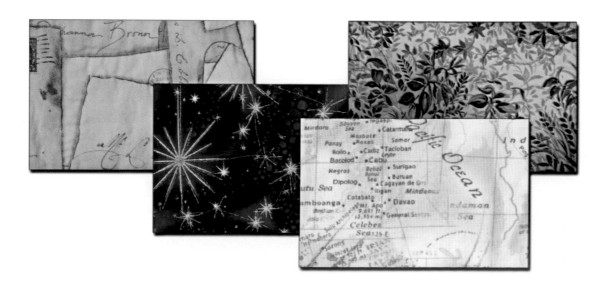

Developing the Story

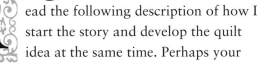

Read the following description of how I start the story and develop the quilt idea at the same time. Perhaps your story and quilt will be entirely different. That's the delight of fairies—they can be anything you want them to be.

Inspiration: Seeing ladybugs in the garden.

Question: Where do ladybugs get their black spots?

Answer: From the beautiful fairie who sits on a smooth garden rock amongst the flowers.

Quilt idea: I see red ladybugs lined up in front of the fairie. She holds a paintbrush and gently paints black spots on them as they walk by. On the other side of her are the painted ladybugs going about their business.

Her dress: Her wings will have black spots and her dress will be red.

Fairie name: Ladybug Fairie

The fairie tale: Twice a year, at the earliest time of the morning, Miss Ladybug Fairie prepares for the

parade of ladybugs eagerly waiting to receive their black spots. She carefully mixes blue and pink sparkles into the potion that makes wishes come true. When each ladybug receives her painted black spots, the gift of luck is also bestowed upon her, allowing mere mortals to make wishes on the ladybug. Little does the person know that, for each unselfish wish on a spot, her hopes and dreams are granted.

Keep your story short and simple. Ask yourself this: If you look at your fairie tale quilt, can you tell the story without seeing the words? And if you read the story, can you envision the quilt? Each one should mirror the other. Remember, it's your story, and you can do anything you want. Fairie tales are for fun, and your story and quilt will be, too.

Quilters and Their Imaginations

One day, while teaching a new fairie appliqué class for the first time, I realized that, by divine intervention, I was assigned a most inventive group of quilters, who had enthusiasm and the attitude of "I can do this."

After each student received her fairie pattern, we showed one another what fabrics we had brought and decided where the best placement for them would be. With that done, everyone eagerly began the glue stick appliqué technique I was there to teach.

As I walked around the classroom, I began to see the differences in each student's fabrics. The fairies' stories began to form in my mind, and for fun, I thought I would ask the quilters to think about names for their fairies. They began to enthusiastically chime in with thoughts on names, and the excitement built. Sometimes the name of the fairie would have to do with the geographical area where the student lived or with the colors and designs in the dress fabrics. What I mainly found out was that each of us has a child within.

Fairie Dust

I want to pass along to you something that allows me the freedom to create. Once you find the thing that makes you feel all giggly and energized to create, make sure you nurture it. This means keeping the thought alive in your mind. The idea may change often, but make sure you don't let it go. Write it down, scribble, doodle, tell someone about it, but don't forget it because you aren't sure about the idea.

Once you have found your idea and you are nurturing the possibilities, by all means keep the inspirations alive. Get out into this big world and breathe in, let your eyes see everything in a new light, and listen for those little muses to cheer you on.

Jump Starters

Once you start to think of a theme for your fairie, the ideas will stream into your mind faster than you can write them down. Everywhere you look, you will begin to think of new ideas and ways to create your stories and quilts. Here are some ideas to jumpstart your own dreams:

Amber Fairie
Shines with beautiful golden amber beads, glistening from sunlight streaming through them.

Baker Fairie
Showers all the cupcakes with sprinkles.

Birthday Fairie
Grants wishes when the candles are blown out.

Bridal Fairie
Ensures the bride has something old, something new, something borrowed, and something blue.

Broadway Fairie
Sits on the edge of the stage and whispers the lines if the actors forget.

Butterfly Fairie
Paints the wings with beautiful colors.

Candlelight Fairie
Places the flicker into the flame.

Candy Fairie
Puts the stripes on peppermint sticks.

Celestial Fairie
Gives the stars their twinkle.

Celtic Fairie
Keeps alive the Irish Fairielore.

Circus Fairie
Gives the clowns their red noses.

Crazy Quilt Fairie
Inspires the decorative stitches.

Diamond Fairie
Sets the sparkle in the stone.

Disco Fairie
Wears lots of glitter and keeps the disco ball turning.

Creating the Fairies

Materials

Are you wondering what kind of fabric you can use to create your fairie? First of all, we know that the traditional face, arms, and legs are usually made in flesh-toned fabrics. If you want to make something out of the ordinary, by all means, try a different color. It is your fairie, and she can be whatever you want her to be.

In some of my classes, students have created the most gorgeous fairies with light blue or green skin, sometimes with a hint of sparkle in them. Think outside of the box and look at your fabric a little differently.

Do not limit yourself to only using 100 percent cotton fabrics. Many crazy-quilt enthusiasts who have joined the FairieGoddessMothers Yahoo group have used velvets and satins in the dresses. But remember, these fabrics may not be appropriate, if you are using the glue-stick appliqué method, because the quilt top will be soaked in water.

Don't forget novelty fabrics. By using the *broderie perse* method (fussy-cutting a design and appliquéing it), you can create the most striking quilt top. Novelty prints can spark your imagination with more ideas. I saw a print with weather vanes on it and suddenly thought that a fairie weather vane would look beautiful. Voila!

Embellishments

Like magpies, fairies are attracted to sparkly things. Embellishments can be important to telling a story or adding some pizzazz to your quilt. Sometimes all it will take is a special charm you have been saving, which you can use on a fairie's necklace. You may be surprised that, just by perusing your embellishments, a story may unfold before your eyes. Consider using charms, beads, yarns, buttons, sequins, paints, specialty threads, metallic tulle, and gems, for starters.

This is a wonderful time for you to show your creativity, perhaps by trying a new embellishment technique or using your fancy stitch work. Beautiful metallic threads can be used to embroider hair instead of appliquéing it. Perhaps you thrive on beading and her dress demands tiny details of beads and ribbon embroidery. There is no limit when it comes to your fairie's world.

Fairie Dust

- I love to talk about my fairie theme ideas with friends because I usually get more ideas to add or a new way to think out a design.

- While sitting, I use a beanbag lapboard to do all my glue-stick appliqué work.

- When I appliqué, I like to rest my hands on a large pillow propped on my lap while I sew.

- Your fairie can be turned into an angel by just redesigning the wings to look less like a butterfly and more like angel wings.

Glue-Stick Appliqué Technique

Glue-stick appliqué is the method I find most useful for my projects. The appliqué pieces can be stitched into units before they are sewn to the background. Sorting the pieces for each unit into little baggies makes for a convenient travel project.

Supplies

fabric for appliqué pieces

background fabric

appliqué needles

thread to match appliqué pieces

freezer paper

black permanent marker

paper scissors

fabric scissors

sharp-pointed embroidery scissors

iron and ironing surface

fine-tipped permanent markers

lap-sized piece of lightweight cardboard

water-soluble glue stick

skewer or toothpick

damp washcloth

masking tape

water-soluble blue marker

thread to match appliqué pieces

fine-tipped permanent markers

warm water

bodkin or tweezers

towel

light box (optional)

small baggies (optional)

Making a Master Copy

Note that asymmetrical patterns are reversed relative to the quilts in the photos, which means that your appliqué templates will be reversed. These reversed templates, when traced on the wrong side of the fabrics, will produce the correct orientation in the finished quilt.

1. If you like to work with small, precise pieces, then there is no need for you to enlarge the design. Use a photocopier to enlarge the design if desired. Create a master copy by tracing directly from the book pattern or from your enlarged design.

2. Make a template copy by taping your master copy to a window or light box. Tape a piece of freezer paper, shiny side down, over your master copy. Trace the pattern by hand on the dull side of the freezer paper with a pencil or a thin black permanent marker. Make sure to add all the dots and any labeling you need.

Overlapping Pieces

3. Look carefully at each design to determine which pieces will overlap one another. A "closed" area is one that must have the seam allowances turned under before being appliquéd. An "open" area does not need to be turned because it will be overlapped by another piece. On the template patterns you will see dots that indicate the open areas. Just think of the dots as little o's for "open" (fig. 1).

Fig. 1. Dots on templates indicate open areas.

4. Cut the template copy pieces apart on the drawn lines with your paper scissors

Cutting Fabric Pieces

5. Place the freezer-paper templates shiny side down on the wrong side of the appropriate fabrics. Press them for a few seconds with a dry, medium-hot iron. Make sure to check that the freezer paper has adhered to the fabric (fig. 2).

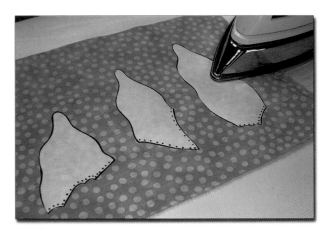

Fig. 2. Press templates onto the wrong side of the fabric.

6. Cut out the fabric pieces, adding a ³⁄₁₆" turn-under allowance around each template. There really is no need to measure exactly, just cut the allowances by eye (fig.3).

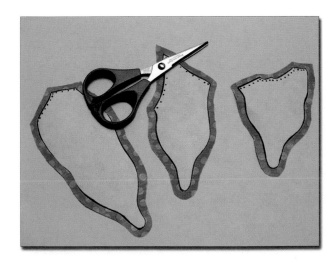

Fig. 3. Leave a ³⁄₁₆" allowance around templates.

7. Clip the inside curves of the closed sections with your embroidery scissors, stopping just short of the turn line.

Turn-Under Allowance

8. Use a piece of lightweight cardboard to keep your working surface clean when using a glue stick. With the appliqué piece wrong side up, lightly spread glue on the allowances along the closed sections (fig. 4).

Fig. 4. Apply glue to the turn-under allowance.

9. Turn the allowances under with a skewer, toothpick, or your fingers (fig. 5). Use a damp washcloth to wipe your fingers clean of any glue residue.

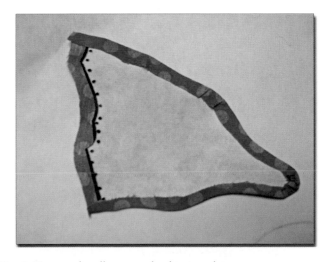

Fig. 5. Turn-under allowance glued to template

Fairie Dust

Details of hands, fingers, chin, etc., can be embroidered or drawn with pens.

Drawing the Face

1. Drawing the face for your fairie is easier than you might imagine. If you are using the glue-stick appliqué method, be sure to draw the face onto the freezer paper when you are tracing your pattern (fig. 6a).

2. After ironing the shiny side of the freezer paper

Fairie Dust

Using a light box or window will improve your ability to see the tiniest details.

template to the fabric, you will be able to see the facial features through the fabric (fig. 6b).

3. Always test your pens on a little scrap of the flesh-tone fabric to make sure you are happy with the results of the colors and the pressure you applied (fig. 7).

Fig. 7. Testing pens

4. Lightly draw the facial features onto the fabric with a light brown fine-tipped permanent pen (fig. 6c).

5. Carefully draw the small details, like eyelashes and little feathered strokes for the eyebrows (fig. 6d).

Fig. 6. (a) Details of face drawn on template, (b) face detail seen through fabric, (c) partially drawn face, (d) completed face.

Stitching the Face
by Bonnie K. Browning

Fig. 9. Outline stitching on the eyes

Instead of painting or drawing the face, I used a single strand of regular sewing thread to stitch the features on the face of Miz Sukey Divine (see page 60).

Here are a few tricks that will help you stitch a face. Choose an embroidery hoop that will secure your fabric. I prefer the No-Slip Hoop because it will hold a single layer of fabric nice and tight. You can also wrap a strip of fabric around the bottom ring of a regular hoop to help hold a single layer tight.

Begin by transferring the design to the fabric. You can use graphite transfer paper. Gray works well and does not leave a heavy line. You can use the colored transfer paper that seamstresses use for marking darts in clothing. A third option is to make a stencil of the face and trace around the cut-out openings.

Using a very small stem or outline stitch (fig. 8) and a single strand of the thread color you will use to fill the spaces, stitch the outer edges of the shapes (fig. 9).

Eyes: A brown thread will outline the eyes without appearing too dark or heavy. Once you have the outline of the eyes finished, stitch the pupil with an eye color. Again, use the outline stitch, but a double strand of thread will fill the space better. Remember to keep your thread on the outside of the arc (fig. 10).

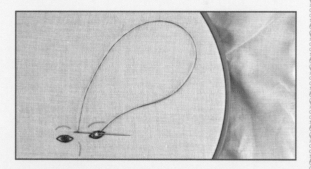

Fig. 10. Stitching of eye in progress

After you have filled the pupil area, make a French knot, wrapping the thread five or six times around the needle (fig. 11). Pull the wrapped thread down tight against the tip of the needle before you pull the thread through.

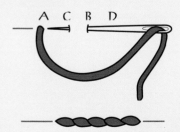

Fig 8. Stem or outline stitch

Remember to consistently keep your thread to the outside arc of curved lines when doing the outline stitch. This will help keep your stitching line smooth.

Fig 11. French knot for the pupil

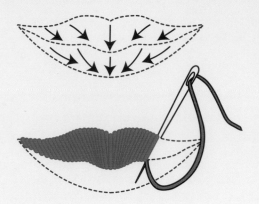

Eyebrows: For the eyebrows, use a single strand of brown thread. Use the outline stitch, but instead of stitching directly on the line, stitch across the line to make the eyebrow wider. Bring the needle up on one side of the line, and take it down on the opposite side of the line (fig. 12).

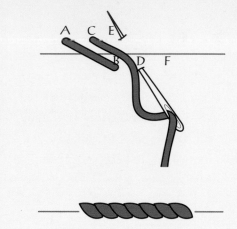

Fig. 12. Angled stem stitch for eyebrow

Eyelashes: Take four or five angled straight stitches along the top and bottom outside corners of the eyes to make eyelashes. The stitches should be longer at the corner and shorter as you work toward the center of the eye.

Lips: The lips will be outlined with a stem stitch and filled in by using a satin stitch and a single strand of thread. The outline stitches will help you keep the shape of the mouth.

Bring the needle up outside the outline stitch, and insert the needle at the opposite edge. Return to the starting line by carrying the thread underneath the fabric. Make stitches close enough together to cover the background fabric completely. Pull the thread until it lies smoothly but does not pucker the background. You are stitching over the outline stitch (fig. 13).

Fig. 13. Stitching the lips

Angling the stitches from the corner of the mouth inward makes it easier to fill the space. When you reach the center of the mouth, angle the stitches vertically, then reverse the angle as you work toward the opposite corner of the mouth. This will make nice sharp corners on the mouth. If you find a small gap between the lips, fill that space by stitching with a single strand of white thread. It will look like teeth. Be sure to take very small stitches so you don't have gaps between the teeth.

Nose: Choose a color of thread slightly darker than the fabric to stitch the nose. Use the outline stitch, taking very small stitches (fig. 14).

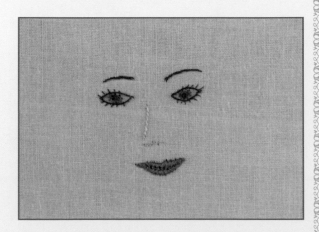

Fig. 14. The finished face

Assembling the Appliqué Units

1. Decide which pieces will be joined as a unit before being appliquéd to the background. For each unit, lightly spread glue on the wrong side of the seam allowance of the appropriate open sections (fig. 15).

Fig. 15. Aligning pieces for a unit

2. Hold the pieces up to a light source, such as a window, light bulb, or a light box to help position them and use your fingers to press the overlapping pieces together. Then appliqué the pieces.

3. Continue adding pieces in this manner until the unit is complete.

Preparing the Background

1. Cut a piece of background fabric an inch or two larger than the size needed for your project.

2. Tape your master copy, pattern side down, to a light box or window. With the master copy right side down, the image will match the orientation of the design in the quilt.

3. Center the background fabric, right side up, on the pattern. Tape the fabric to the light box or window and, with a thin water-soluble blue

marker, lightly trace the pattern onto the fabric. This tracing is a placement guide for the appliquéd units, so you need not mark every detail (fig. 16).

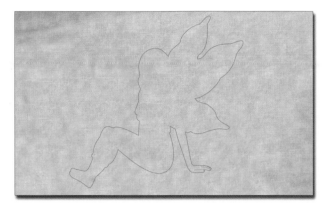

Fig. 16. Placement lines on the background fabric help position appliqué.

4. Using the traced lines on the background fabric for reference, appliqué your units to the background.

5. Cut out the background fabric from behind the appliquéd pieces, leaving a ³⁄₁₆" allowance.

Removing the Freezer Paper

1. After the final appliqué has been sewn down, soak the entire piece in lukewarm water and agitate slowly with your hands or, using a bucket of water and a clean sponge, slowly dab appliqué sections to loosen the freezer paper.

2. Gently remove all the loosened freezer paper with a bodkin, tweezers, or your fingers.

3. Drain the used water, refill your sink, and dip the piece in clean water. Gently squeeze the excess water out by hand, but do not twist the fabric. Roll the quilt top in a thick towel to remove more water.

4. Gently steam-press the appliqué top, right side down, on a clean dry towel. Turn the piece over and lightly press again.

Rainbow Fairie
Painter of Color, Hopes, and Dreams

Story and quilt by the author; quilting by Judy Irish

Every day is a rainbow day in the life of a rainbow Fairie.

Painting the rainbow with beauty and light,
Arching the sky, a magical sight.

Silver-lined clouds of enormous height
Give this Fairie sheer delight.

She holds her paintbrush nice and tight,
Filling the colors over bias-taped white.

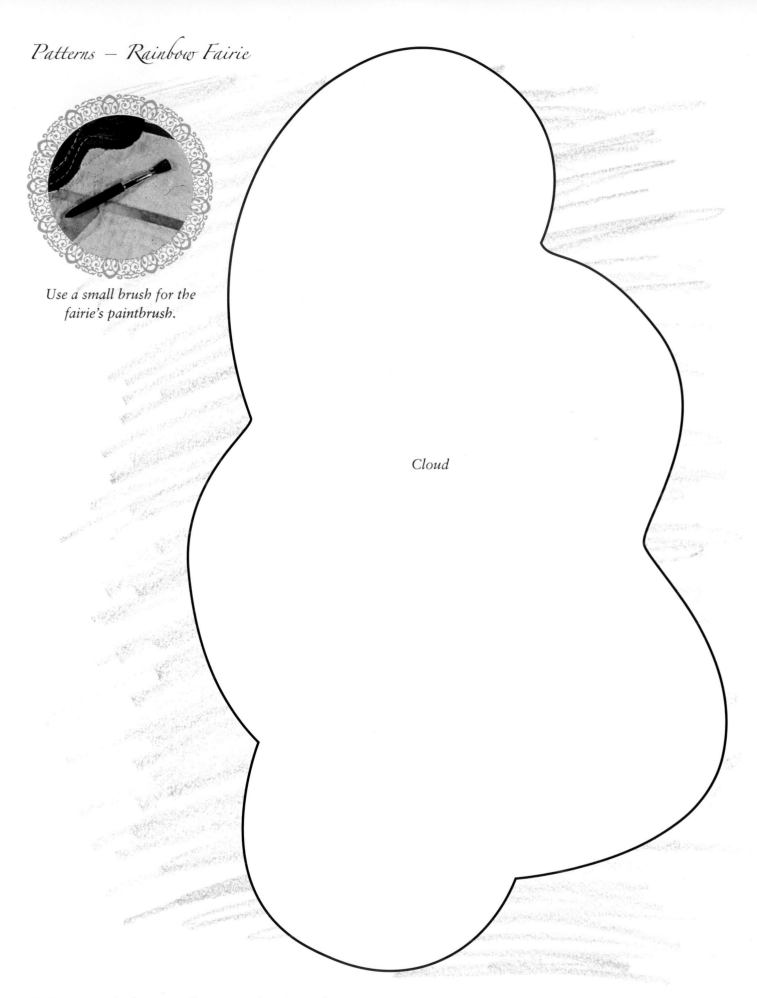

Use a small brush for the
fairie's paintbrush.

Cloud

Butterfly Fairie

Story and quilt by the author; quilting by Judy Irish

Whenever the Butterfly Fairie is close by, butterflies can feel she is there. Excitement builds as they journey to see her. They know that they will soon be given their special colored wings. As her arms open for the colorful ceremony, she says,

"Spread your wings
So I may see
The colors I will
Give to thee.

Protect them
In every way
And spread your joy
Each brand new day."

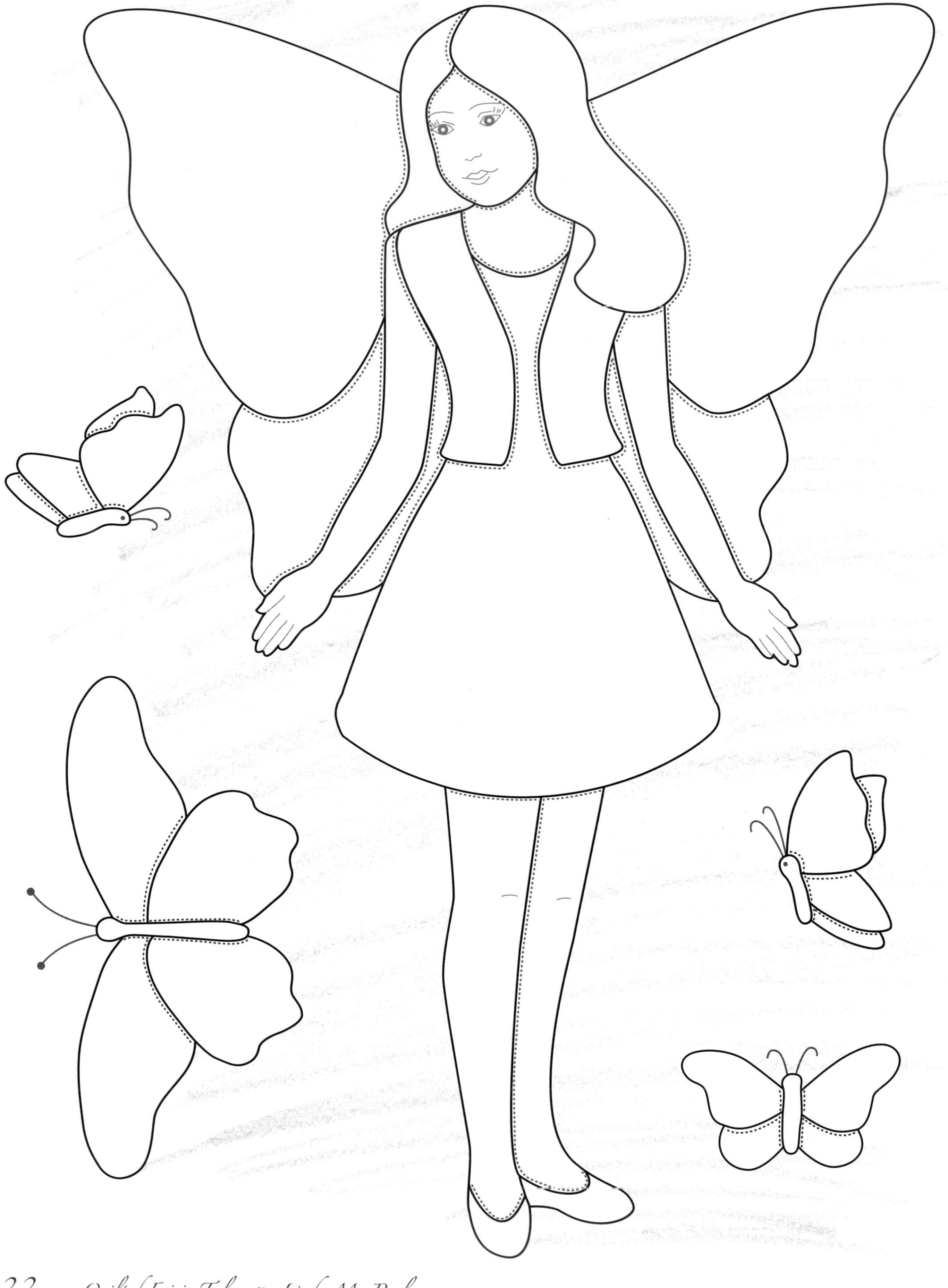

Tippy Toes

Story and quilt by the author; quilting by Judy Irish

Tippy Toes waits each night
To make sure
The moon shines bright.
And when the crescent isn't right,
She flies above to fix the light.
And if the tilt doesn't stay,

She tips her toes
And waits till day.
So when you see
A crooked moon,
Rest assured
Tippy Toes will be there soon!

Flip and trace to draw the other half of the moon.

Annie Oakleaf

Story and quilt by the author; quilting by Judy Irish

"Hurry, Annie, hurry!" said Autumn Squirrel. "The acorns are falling, and I need your help to gather them." The baby squirrel ran circles around her and occasionally stopped to catch a falling leaf. Annie Oak Leaf smiled at the excitement of her little furry friend. It was her most favorite time of year.

Valentina

Fairie of Love Letters

Story by the author; quilt and quilting by Helen Umstead, Hawley, Pennsylvania

With pen to paper by candlelight,
Words appear on the full-moon night.

The roses are red and the violets are blue
She'll help you write, "I Love You."

And as you seal your heartfelt love letter
Her magical spell makes you feel better.

She assures that all your words will be read
And words are better than what could be said.

So remember this fairie will always appear
When love's in the air, be it far or quite near.

Embellish the hearts
with lace and beads.

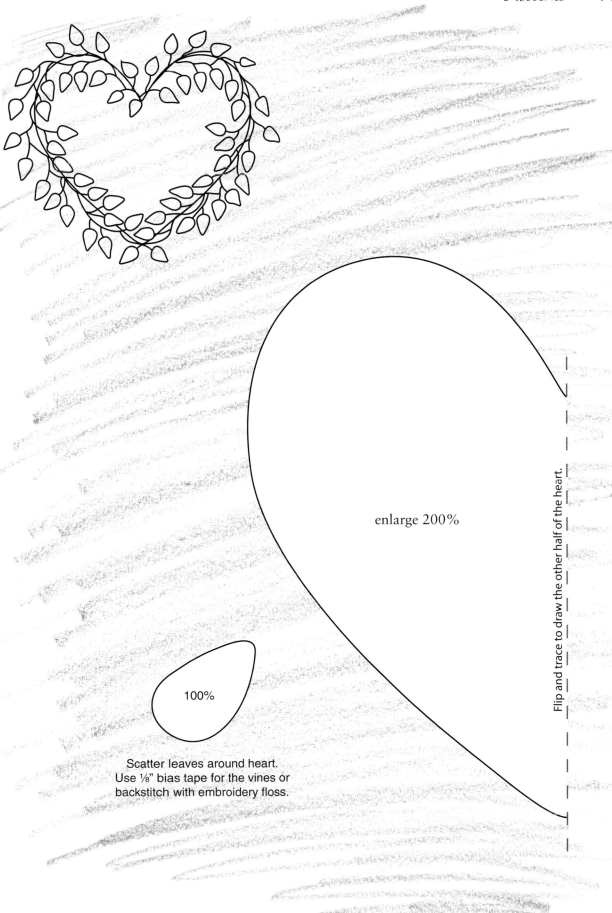

enlarge 200%

Flip and trace to draw the other half of the heart.

100%

Scatter leaves around heart.
Use ⅛" bias tape for the vines or
backstitch with embroidery floss.

Valentina

Honey, the Bee Keeper

Butterfly Fairie

Fire Fairie

Rainbow Fairie

Fairie Wing Flyer

Annie Oakleaf

Ladybug Fairie

Fairie Princess Joy

Flower Fairie

Tippy Toes

Honey, the Bee Keeper

Story and quilt by the author; quilting by Judy Irish. Corner squares are Honey Bee blocks.

At the edge of the garden, Honey, the Bee Keeper, can hear her small honeybee friends humming from flower to flower. Her little friends work hard every day gathering nectar and pollen to bring home. Sometimes they work so hard they forget to come home on time.

Thankfully, their special fairie knows exactly when they have gathered enough and calls them home each evening. Inside their beehive home is the honeycomb where the honey and pollen are stored. Each morning their guardian fairie is given a piece of bread smothered in the sweetest honey on earth as thanks for her protection.

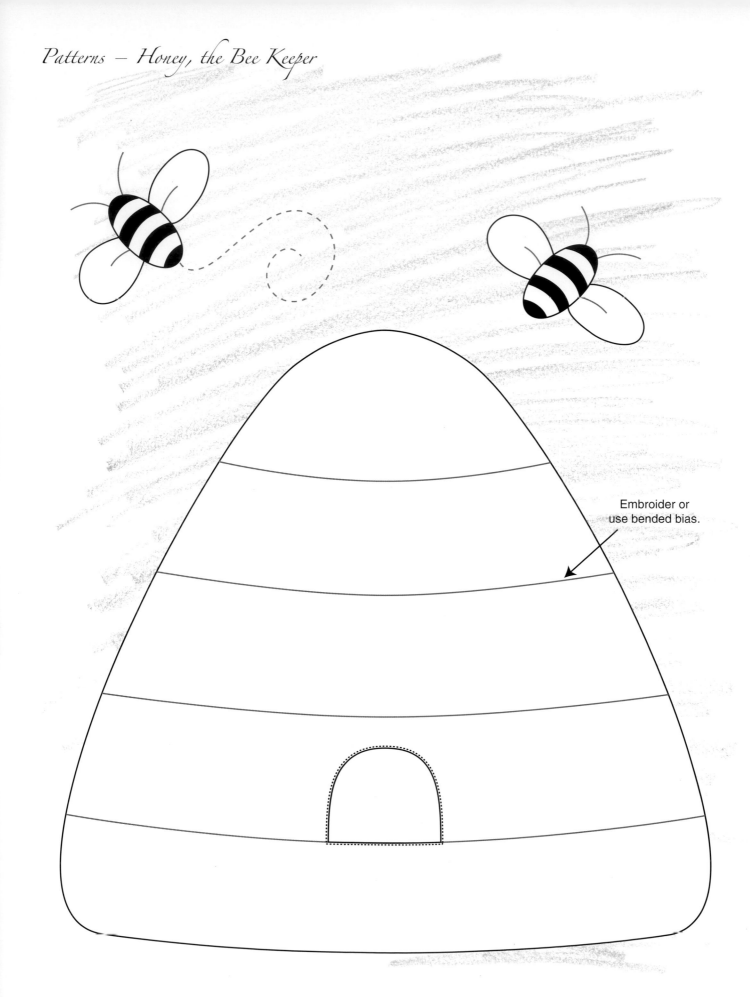

Embroider or
use bended bias.

Fairie Wing Flyer

Story and quilt by the author; quilting by Judy Irish

On the back roads of Bird House Lane, Fairie Wing Flyer
was getting ready to launch the first flight of the newest
baby birds. Her teaching was much like how her parents
taught her as a young fairie: To fly, just follow Mom and
Pop and run like the wind 'til your wings catch the breeze,
then glide. Birds of the world so loved and trusted her
that, everywhere she went to teach, graduate birds
came to cheer on the newest students.

Today, the fledglings try out their wings as
their parents proudly watch.

Use quilting to add
woodgrain detail to the tree.

Use bias tape
or embroider.

Ladybug Fairie

Story and quilt by the author; quilting by Judy Irish

Twice a year, early in the morning, Miss Ladybug Fairie prepares for the parade of ladybugs eagerly waiting to receive their black spots. She carefully mixes blue and pink sparkles into a potion that makes wishes come true. As each ladybug receives her painted black spots, the gift of luck is bestowed, allowing any mere mortal to make wishes on them. Little do the people know that for each unselfish wish on a spot, their hopes and dreams will be granted!

Use fabric paint or a
permanent marker for the
ladybug spots and legs.

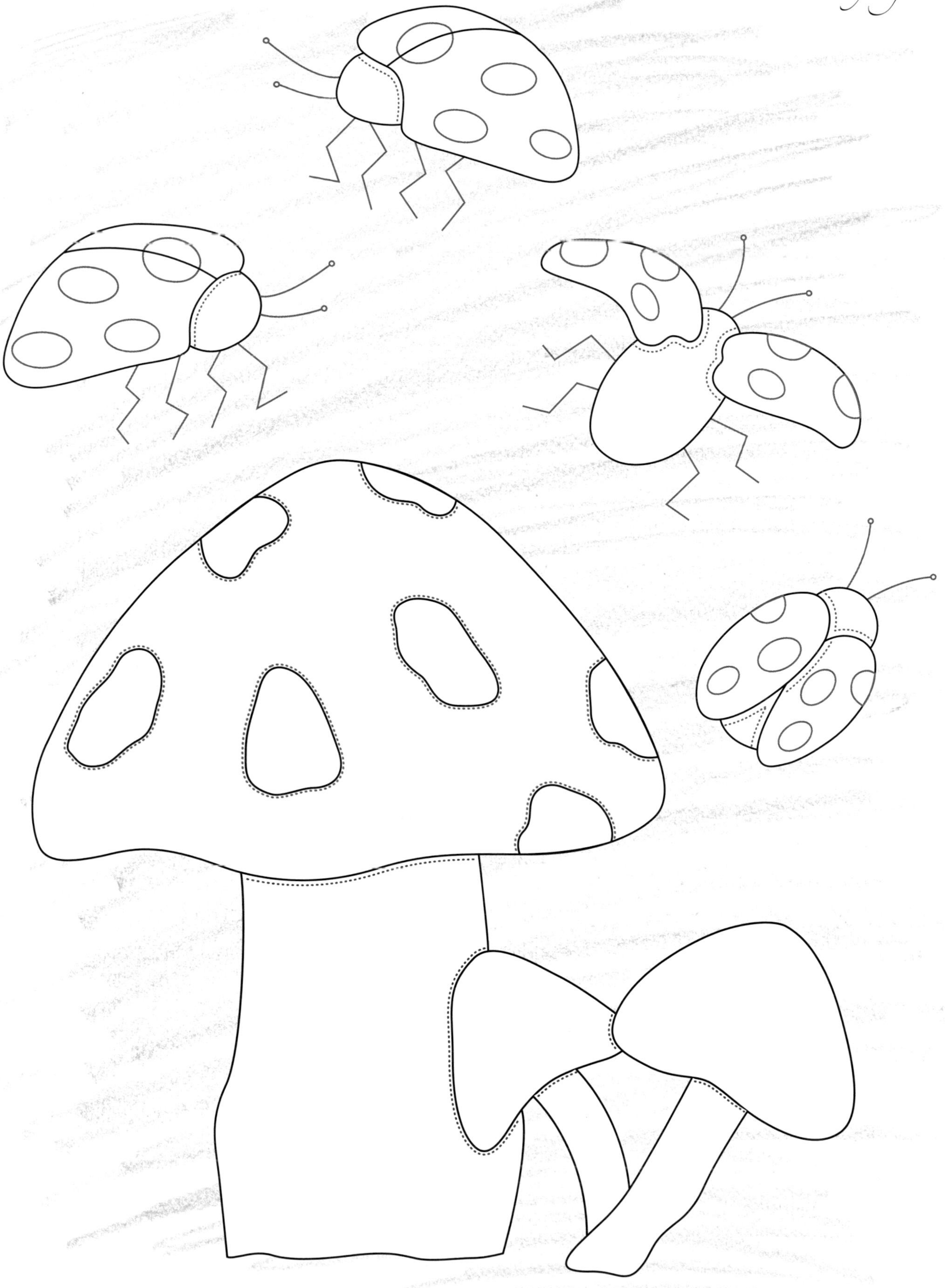

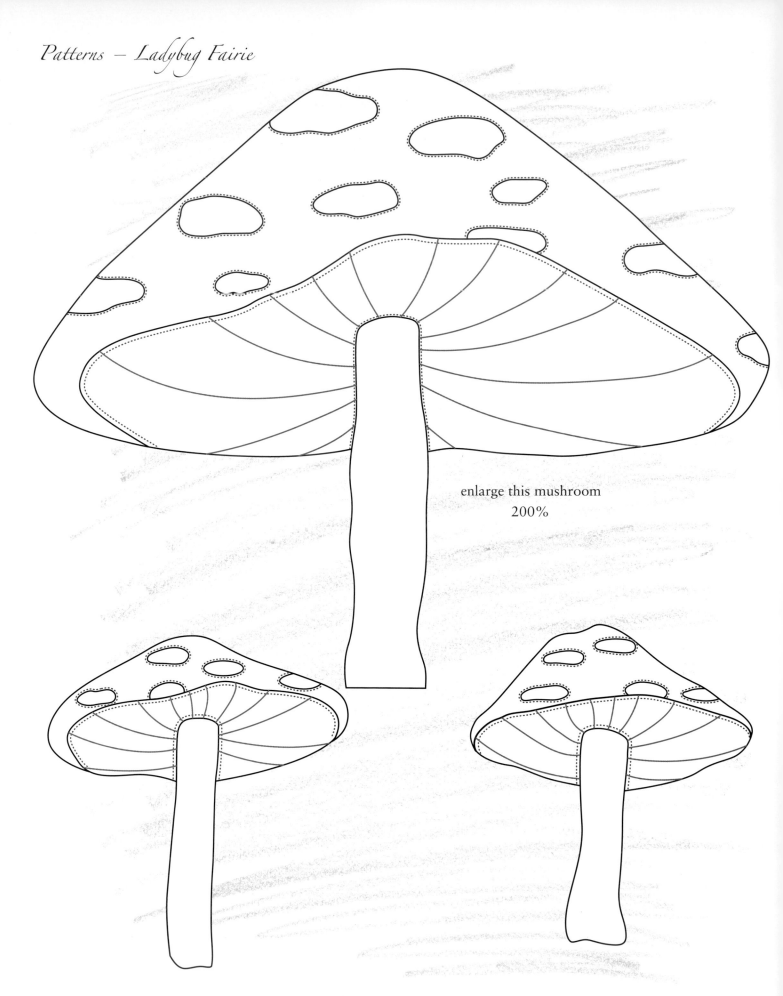

enlarge this mushroom
200%

Flower Fairie

Story and quilt by the author; quilting by Judy Irish

Sometimes, in the very early mornings of spring, just when the sun begins to rise, you can catch the quick glimmer of a tiny fairie dancing and singing in the garden. She tries to be ever so quiet, but her heart fills with love as she sees her beautiful posies sleeping. Her songs and dance calmly wake the sleepy flowers for another beautiful day of color.

So, if you are lucky enough to see the Flower Fairie one morning, listen closely and you may hear her sing:

"The sun is rising   Shine your colors   Bow your heads
This brand new day,   With pure delight   When daytime ends
Lift your heads   For all to see   And I'll be back
This month of May.   In this sunlight.   To sing again."

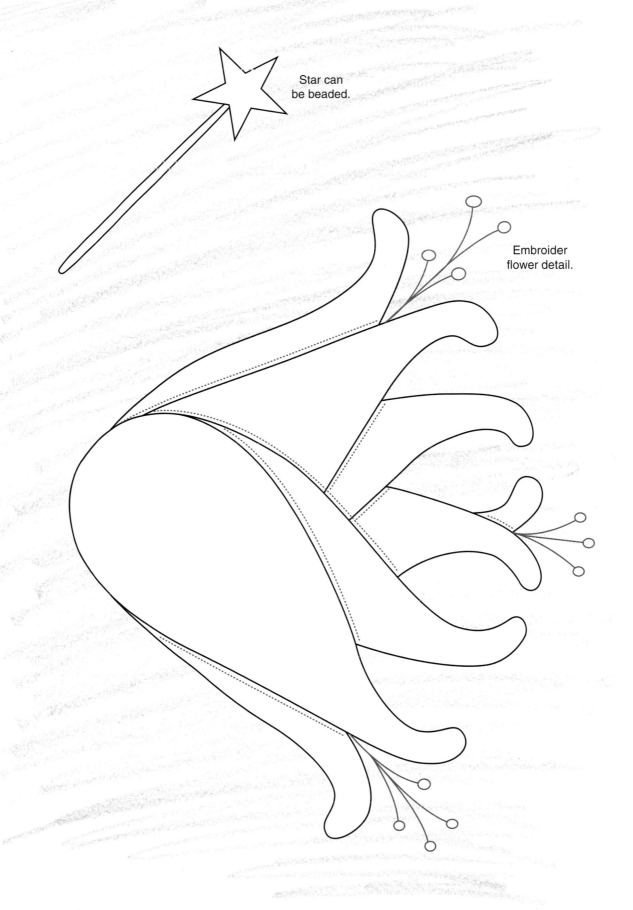

Star can
be beaded.

Embroider
flower detail.

Fire Fairie

"Now puff and puff and puff once more
And exhale slowly on the count of four,"
Fire Fairie told her students. One little purple dragon just couldn't get it right and was embarrassed. "I just can't! It comes out wrong, and it isn't even red fire. It comes out in colors," he said. The other dragons giggled because they had never heard of such a thing.

Soon it was his time to show what he had learned. He was embarrassed and couldn't spit a spark if he tried. The Fire Fairie said, "Close your eyes; concentrate on your breath." As he closed his eyes, he could hear the class laughing. His lungs filled with air, and as he exhaled, he could feel the heat burst forth. The class ahhhh'ed and applauded. With his head down, he asked if he had passed the test.

Story by the author; quilt by Gloria Grohs, Milford, Pennsylvania; quilting by Judy Irish

"Not only is that the best flame I have ever seen," the teacher said, "but only once in every one hundred years do I see a dragon who breathes the colors worthy of being fireworks." After class, the other dragons asked forgiveness for making fun of his little flame. Now their Kingdom was a magical kingdom, one with a fireworks-breathing dragon!

enlarge 300%

*Use quilting to add
scales to the dragon.*

enlarge 300%

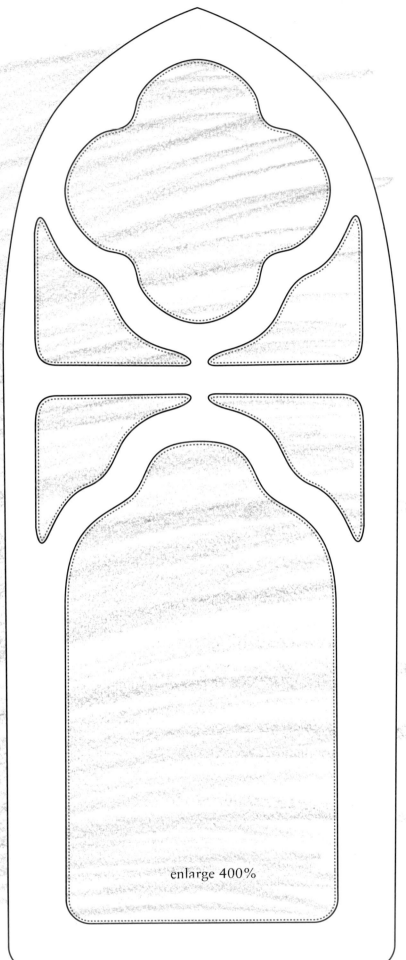

enlarge 400%

Fairie Princess Joy,
the Once-Upon-a-Time Fairie

The most beautiful castle in the land sat high upon the hills of the Kingdom Scribe. On the morning of the full moon, Fairie Princess Joy flew over the hills where the children of other kingdoms patiently waited.

The children knew that, when they saw her, they could fly with her to her magical kingdom. Not many knew that the Kingdom of Scribe was where every single fairie tale was born. The people, known as Scribonians, dreamed and created the most magnificent tales ever written.

Story by the author; quilt by the author and Helen Umstead, Hawley, Pennsylvania; quilting by Judy Irish

At the end of each play day (Scribonians never, ever use the word "work"), they brought to Fairie Princess Joy their beautiful finished stories. With quill in hand, she dipped the point into the ink bottle. Speaking the words as she wrote, the children eagerly recited along with her: "Once upon a time…." and the new stories of the moon cycle were told.

If you believe in fairie tales, you will know that, once upon a time, there lived a fairie princess named Joy whose job was to script the beginning words to every fairie tale!

enlarge 200%

Extra Accessories

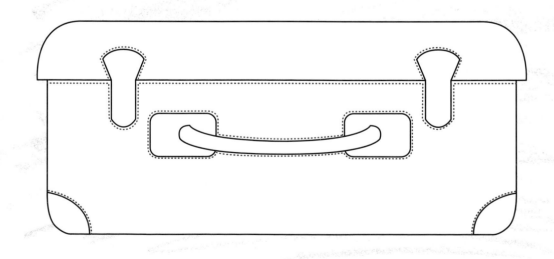

Fairie Variations
BOO! the Halloween Fairie

Story by Alison Rumble, Kingston-Upon-Hull, England;
quilt design and quilting by the author;
quilt by Alison, the author, and Helen Umstead, Hawley, Pennsylvania

As the cold wind blew fiercely in the valley of Halloween Hill, the beautiful fairie rubbed her arms for warmth and tried to protect her wings from freezing. In the light of the full moon, she saw her friend Elvira, a black cat with almond-shaped blue eyes. Boo never grew tired of hearing Elvira tell how the fairie came to be. So the cat cuddled into her lap and told this story:

Sitting on the porch steps, a little girl worked hard to scoop out the insides of a pumpkin. Only a pair of blue eyes was watching her. The little girl wished for a friend to share in her efforts, and tears fell down her face onto the pulp at her feet. The next day, a single seed started to grow from the little girl's tears. A new pumpkin grew, bigger and stronger than any other.

The blue-eyed cat instinctively guarded the orange orb as it grew, knowing how precious it was. One day, her whiskers started to twitch as the pumpkin suddenly broke open. There on the ground was a beautiful, tiny creature, flapping her wings like a butterfly fresh from a chrysalis. As the little fairie had surprised Elvira, the feline named her Boo!

Signorina Gloriana Fabia, the Carnival Fairie of Venice

Quilt design and story by the author;
quilt by Gloria Grohs, Milford, Pennsylvania; quilting by Judy Irish

Every year, on the night before Lent begins, Signorina Gloriana drifts through the mists rising up from the canals and enshrouding the grand buildings of Venice, Italy.

Tonight, she rides in her golden gondola that will bring her to the Piazza San Marco, where there will be parties, some official and some private. For her, the beauty of Carnivale is that no one is better than anyone else.

She attends Carnivale to ensure that each person wears a mask, thereby disguising their social status, so all can attend the best of the best celebrations!

Hanachan, the Kimono Fairie

Story and quilt by Jennifer O'Brien, Westbury, Connecticut

Hanachan lives in the Kyoto Gardens in Japan. Her name translates to Flower Child. She loves the flowers in the garden. Each season in the garden brings out a different style of kimono. Hanachan loved the kimono and the way it represents the seasons through depictions of flowers and other natural elements. She loved to see the kimonos, but in Japan today, western-style clothing is the dress of choice.

This worried Hanachan. Year after year she saw fewer and fewer kimonos, so she decided it was time she did something about it. She would become the keeper of the kimono tradition. Hanachan realized that the younger generation would have to save the tradition. She was happy when adults brought their children to see her garden. She would fly up to a child's shoulder when the parents weren't looking and tell them of the kimono tradition.

She would tell them to ask their parents for a kimono and encourage them to learn the fine points of wearing the kimono. Hanachan would also appear to anyone wearing a kimono in the garden. She would invite them to return as often as possible, dressed in kimonos so the children could see how lovely a kimono is to wear. If you would like Hanachan to come to you, just wear a kimono to the Kyoto Gardens.

Ivanna Travel, the First Class Fairie

Story and quilt by the author; quilting by Judy Irish

I am told that a fairie has been seen in my company when I travel. At first I was amused when people told me this, thinking it was just their way of wishing me good luck. With the amount of traveling I do, I never pay much attention to the peacefulness that washes over me when the seat belt sign turns off and my eyes close for a nap.

It was that one particular flight—you know, the one with turbulence like a roller coaster—when I felt the breeze of a tiny little flutter and looked down to my right hand clenching the armrest.

There she was, smiling at me, a little golden-haired fairie. She ever so gently flew to my shoulder and whispered in my ear, "It's all right, just a change of weather. I've been with you on every trip, taking care of you."

Amazingly, at that point, the turbulence stopped, seatbelt signs turned off, and chatter among the passengers resumed. When I asked her name, she smiled and told me, "My name is Ivanna, Ivanna Travel." I smiled, because I remembered telling everyone when I was young, "I want to travel. Yes, I want to travel!"

Payden, the Pirate Fairie

Story by Phoebe H. Guider;
quilt by Phoebe and Joyce R. Hartley, Richmond, Virginia

Payden the Pirate,
That's what she was called.
She plundered and plundered;
All were enthralled.

Her name was well known.
All lived in fear
That one day they might hear
Her battle cry near.

There was never a battle
She was afraid to fight.
She fought and she fought,
'Til victory was in sight.

Her true love was the sea,
Where she truly belonged.
Her heart was in her sails,
Where it could never be wronged.

Payden the Pirate,
Whose name was well known,
Shall always be remembered,
And none shall take her throne.

Miz Sukey Divine

Story and quilt by Bonnie K. Browning, Paducah, Kentucky;
quilting by Irene Reising, Paducah, Kentucky

There once was a gal named Sukey Divine, who grew up in the 1950s when words had totally different meanings. She knew that "bread" was money, "threads" were clothes, "nest" was a hairdo, and "drag" was a short car race.

Smokey the Bear gained national prominence, PaperMate® produced the first leak-proof ballpoint pen, Elvis made his first recording, and Paul Harvey began his radio broadcasts. Mr. Potato Head®, Play-Doh®, Barbie®, and hula hoops all arrived. It was the era of *American Bandstand*, blue jeans, and poodle skirts.

For Sukey, it was a time of working in the family diner and driving around town in her shiny, black Corvette rag top. She used her creativity to make her clothes, in pinks and purples. Even though Clairol® introduced their "Does She or Doesn't She?" campaign, there is no doubt what Miz Sukey has been doing to her hair.

Now that you know a little bit about Miz Sukey Divine, it's time to split (leave), so punch it (step on the gas), or we'll miss the latest episode of *The Donna Reed Show*. Later, Gator!

Jewel's Woods

Story and quilt by Diann E. Becker,
Shohola, Pennsylvania

There once was a fairie named Jewel who was named for the sparkle in her eyes. She lived in Briar Patch Hollow, which was the most beautiful woods.

Jewel loved the fresh air, the chirping birds, and the clear water of the pond where the animals would come to drink.

The other fairies taught Jewel the secrets of Briar Patch Hollow—secrets that must be kept hidden from mortals who would cut down the trees and remove the homes of the animals. They would fill in the pond, calling it a swamp, so they could build their homes and shopping centers.

Only the mortal whose soul is true, who will protect the hollow with everything within him, will see the beauty of life and the riches there. And with that thought, Jewel would go to sleep, dreaming of the secrets of her hollow.

If you find yourself in the woods, take notice of the beauty in the crystal clear streams and the fragrance of a rare flower. Stop and listen to the life living there and the bells ringing in the distance. Or is that fairie music you hear?

Resources

Linda M. Poole
113 7th Street #15
Milford, PA 18337
E-mail: linda@lindampoole.com
Web site: www.lindampoole.com

Clotilde
Notions catalog
Phone: 800-772-2891
Web site: www.clotilde.com

Petal Play
Appli-Bond© supplies
102 Courtney Road
Harwich, MA 02645
Phone: 508-430-0347
Web site www.petalplay.com

The Appliqué Society
PO Box 89
Sequim, WA 98382-0089
E-mail: tas@theappliquesociety.org
Web site: www.theappliquesociety.org

Quilter's Attic
Fabrics, notions, quilting supplies
PO Box 1592, Route 302
Pine Bush, NY 12566
Phone: 845-744-5888
Web site: www.quiltersattic.com

Wild Irish Rows
Long Arm Quilting
Judy Irish
24533 35th Ave. N.E.
Arlington, WA 98223
Phone: 360-403-4868
E-mail: wildirishrows@yahoo.com

Katie Lane Quilts
Radial Rules™ and Thread Wrap®
PO Box 1240
Amherst, NH 03031-2554
Phone: 603-673-2867
Web site: www.katielane.com

The FairieGoddessMothers Internet Group
http://groups.yahoo.com/group/fairiegoddessmothers/

Linda M. Poole is an enthusiastic appliqué artist whose laughter and humor are contagious in both the classroom and lecture halls. She mentors those she teaches with patience and a firm belief that "they can do it." Non-appliquérs walk out of her classes convinced that indeed they can.

Now, with the birth of her fairies, she leads a network of FairieGoddessMothers from all over the world who delight in creating fairies and their stories. You, too, can join the fun at http://groups.yahoo.com/group/fairiegoddessmothers/.

Linda comes from a long line of artists, watercolorists, impressionists, stained glass artisans, weavers, sculptresses, silversmiths, and winemakers—all things that make for "The Good Life!"

She lives in the gorgeous Pocono Mountains region of northeastern Pennsylvania in the small town of Milford, known for its eclectic community of artists and antique shops. Linda has a passion for traveling the globe, learning from those she meets, and passing forward everything she learns.

Linda M. Poole is the author of the popular books *Turkish Delights to Appliqué* and *Bended Bias Appliqué*. She can be reached through her Web site, www.lindampoole.com, or by e-mailing her at linda@lindampoole.com.

Other AQS Books

This is only a small selection of the books available from the American Quilter's Society. AQS books are known worldwide for timely topics, clear writing, beautiful color photos, and accurate illustrations and patterns. The following books are available from your local bookseller, quilt shop, or public library.

#7010   us$21.95

#7016   us$22.95

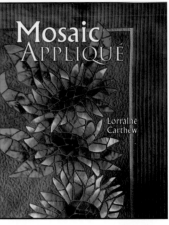

#7071   us$22.95

#6511   us$22.95

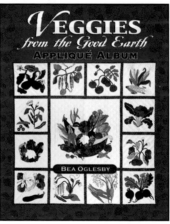

#7017   us$21.95

#6903   us$19.95

#7075   us$22.95

#6904   us$21.95

#6897   us$22.95

LOOK for these books nationally. **CALL 1-800-626-5420**
or **VISIT** our Web site at **www.AmericanQuilter.com**